Take A Deep Breath

Finding What Hope Means To You

Dr. Angela Charles

Made with ❤ on the BookLeaf Publishing Platform
www.bookleafpub.in
www.bookleafpub.com

Dedication

I dedicate this book of poetry to my husband, parents, sons, and my beautiful granddaughter Danica whose unwavering love and support have been the foundation and reason for my journey. Their encouragement to pursue my dreams has inspired me to write and share my stories with the world and lovers of poetry, family, and hope everywhere. This dedication is a tribute to their faith, hope, sacrifices and the countless lessons they have taught me about resilience and kindness and never giving up on a dream.

Love you guys with my whole heart. This one is in honor of you Mom. I miss you every single day and pray you know the love and hope you left behind in all of our lives. Your sacrifice is seen in all of us! May you find joy and peace in the most beautiful place God ever created. Even though Heaven is your home now, I still have the HOPE to see you again some day!

Preface

In the preface of the poetry book, the author, Dr. Angela Charles, poignantly sets the stage for future readers by providing real poems that are true and entangled in the emotions and life the author has lived to date. The personal anecdotes shared create an emotional connection, inviting you into the author's world and demonstrating the relevance of hope for many being the only thing that can be seen as a constant. Additionally, the use of vivid language and clear structure enhances the experiences explored in each poem, making them engaging and informative. Truly, the author hopes they will help someone, somewhere, roll through the waves of grief, find hope in family, and love the very essence of this wild and wonderful life we have been given. Keep Hope Alive!

Acknowledgements

In her book, *Take A Deep Breath: Finding What Hope Means To You*, Dr. Angela Charles masterfully weaves poems of hope amidst some moments of joy and despair. The poems envelope her life as a youngster in the Appalachian Mountains and an adult in North Carolina. The poetry follows a young girl whose journey to adulthood helps her find solace in her family, reading and research, and her 24 years as an educator. Throughout the poetry, Angela's relationships with her parents, husband, sons, granddaughter, and students illustrate even in the more difficult of times, love and kindness can and does prevail. The recurring motif of words and stories serves as a powerful reminder that hope can be found in the most unexpected places. Charles' poignant poetry and unique perspectives encourage readers to reflect on the resilience of the human spirit, making her poetry a profound exploration of hope and finding the light at the end of tunnels that life causes you to need to traverse.

1. Glimmer of Hope

In the darkest portion of a night, a star will gleam,
A whisper of light, helping to acknowledge a distant
hope or dream.
Through storms we waiver and wander, through
struggles and trials we tend to roam,
Hope is the part of our heart that leads us in our perfect
direction toward home.
With every heartbeat and sparkle of hope, a promise we
keep,
In the treacherous valley of shadows, where tears often
flow and sorrows seep.
It lifts us higher and allows us to soar above troublesome
matters, like a bird in flight,
Hope paints the horizon and new dawn with colors ever-
so bright.
When the road that we journey on seems winding and
long, and the path unclear,
Hope is the inner voice that we triumphantly hold dear.
It sings to our very soul and hearts, a melody oh so
sweet,

A reminder of strength in the face of what some
struggles meant to be defeat.
So, forever hold on to the peace and dreams of hope, let
it guide you on your way,
Through the darkest of nights ever inching toward the
brightest of a new day.
For in every struggle or bump along the trip, in every
fight or discontenting moment,
Hope is the eternal flame that ignites our fire to live and
always pursue the sweetness of the light.

2. Faith of a Child

In the deep, dark depths where movement stirs clouds of
dust and smoke and men must crawl and creep,
Fear whispers softly beneath all those miles of rock,
there are secrets it must keep.
A miner's heart beats with a sound of picks and shovels
that ring loud and true,
Amidst the black, silent darkness, prayers from a child's
faith shines through.
Each strike of the pick, a young girl's prayer goes toward
the heavens in the stillness of the night,
Guiding the souls of those weary workers with a
peaceful, flickering light.
Though the earth may tremble, and the walls may break
forth in a sigh,
With hope in our hearts and love for fellow man, we
reach for the sky.
Beneath the weight of stone, men work together to
provide the world the coal it needs- amidst much strife,
No matter the cost, we find our strength, our will to
survive and keep our life.

No obstacle is too great, no treacherous condition too
vast, pushing aside every fear that darkens the way,
Faith and prayers from all those we love will provide
hope and the lantern to help us journey toward a new
day.

Honoring the hard work of our Coal Miners... I am a
Coal Miner's Daughter.

3. Hope and Family

A humbled home and family found love in the heart of
our shared laughter,
Where whispers of hope, hardwork and dreams softly
play,
Family's warmth wraps around us all even into the
hereafter,
Guiding us through moment after moment of each
passing day.
Through storms and shadows of trouble yet to come, we
gather,
In unity and prayer, we rise through the good and bad
and manage to stand tall,
With dreams and hopes woven together like threads of
intricate design,
Together, we conquer, we support, we solve problems,
and in unity, we rise and fall.
Our family focuses on hope being the light that ignites
our very spirits,
A beacon that shines in the dark awaiting us to strive to
answer the call,

In family, we find our foundation, the very place where
me meet and face our limits,
A familial love that forever leaves a mark and a place to
hold enough love for us all.

4. Hope is Real

Hope is a flickering flame that keeps warmth and dreams
alive,
In the darkest nights it glows with a beautiful light that
gleams,
A whisper in the silence causes people to wonder why
the flame sometimes will dim,
A promise in our lives slips through the cracks toward
broken dreams.
Hope will shine again someday and bring a lift to our
weary spirits,
With wings that soar away from shadows of doubt
toward the heavens on high,
Love and joy builds a bridge across the shadows of doubt
and lost hope,
Giving us all a true and very real reason not to cry.
Through storms it stands tall, resilient against the forces
that are meant to diminish its strength,
A beacon to show the world the dreams that come true
and hope that lives on shining bright,
In every heart it lingers, and allows for a life worth

living.

A guide through life and a hope through what seems to be an endless night.

5. Making Hope Happen

In the dawn's soft effervescent glow, we rise to become
anew,
With dreams as our compass, they will guide us and see
us through.
Hope is a whisper, a spark on the 4th of July that
permeates the night,
Guiding our hearts with its gentle, yet piercing light.
With often supernatural courage we gather together,
hand in hand,
Growing together moment by sacred moment, together
we will stand.
Through many trials and storms and life's decisions, our
unified spirits will soar,
For hope is always in the form of a promise, an open
door.

6. Teaching Hope

In the walls of a classroom's embrace, where dreams take flight,
Each lesson creates a beacon, casting away the confusion of night.
With words planted like seeds, we harvest in their little growing minds,
Hope blossoms in hearts, leaving doubts left far behind.
We nurture with kindness and love their spirits, through struggles, doubts and fears,
With patience and kindness, we work to dry all their tears.
Every mistake is a step along the way,
Toward the gaining of knowledge and strength, in the light of every new school day.
Together we rise, hand in hand protecting one another, side by side,
In the journey of learning, we take great pride.
So here's to all the teachers, who provide a light and become a champion and diminish the dark,

Igniting the future, with the perfect mix of hope in each
little spark.

11

7. Hope is an Emotional Science

Hope is an emotional science,
A whimper or whisper in the darkest hour,
It nurtures ones' dreams with gentle experienced hands,
And turns our fears to a frail yet fragile flower.
Within the deepest depths of sorrow's swift tide,
Hope rises with loyalty just like the morning sun,
Every heartbeat reverberates with echoes, resiliently strong and bright,
A testament that we are all in this together as one.
In every tear, a seed of positive hope is sown,
With care, it grows through storms, life's upsets and strife,
A compass yielding to the elements and still able to guide us back home,
The emotional science of hope will forever pierce the darkness and work to Illuminate our paths of life.

8. Saying Hello To Your Future Hope

As dawn breaks, the new me will greet the sun,
A whisper of new dreams has just begun.
With every surrendered step, I begin to chase the light,
My future hope beckons in the distance, bold and bright.
Hope dances lightly through the trees while riding on
the breeze,
In every challenge, I find grace which brings me to my
knees.
With open arms, I am grateful to be able to embrace the
day,
For tomorrow's promise forever grasps hold of me and
guides my way.
The road ahead may provide many twists and bends,
But with each turn, I will continue to find favor and
ascend.
So here I am so full of love and hope where I stand, with
my heart aglow,
Saying hello to the future of which I recognize as good I
know.

9. Hope Versus Fear

In dreadful shadows deep, where fears do go to creep,
Hope flickers ever so softly, a light to keep.
Through unexpected stormy nights and awful, endless
dread,
It whispers and nudges gently for us to try to move on
ahead.
With every fresh new day's dawn, an exciting chance
reborn,
Fear may grip and bind, but hope gracefully adorns.
A heart once reluctantly heavy, now yearns and
patiently learns to soar,
In hope's embrace, we have no tightly clutched grip and
thus fear no more.

10. Hope Costs Nothing

In the quiet nature of day, hope whispers soft,
A light breaking through the clouds, lifting spirits aloft.
No currency will be spent, yet many riches will unfold,
In the warmth feeling of belief, in the brave and the bold.
When shadows loom and continue to grow large, and
dreams seem to start to fade,
Hope is the unseen anchor, a promise that is forever
being remade.
It costs the world nothing, yet what it provides us is
priceless as it grows,
In a mere heartbeat of courage, its true power display
always shows.

11. Power of Hope and Spiritual Truth

In the shadows of uncertainties of the night,
Where darkness tries to dim my inner light.
I hold on to the very hope, a spiritually tight embrace,
Believing in something beyond what I see in this place.

Hope is my true anchor, truth will always be my guide,
Lifting my inner spirit where peace will need to reside.
Stronger than doubt, and so much deeper than fear,
A infinitely sacred connection that always feels as if it is drawing near.

Every single struggle, each and every challenge I might face,
Will reveal a wisdom, a divine and much needed saving grace.
The journey isn't measured by what the things that my eyes can see,
But, by the very substantial faith burning from within me.

Spiritual truth always whispers in my ear so very soft
and clear,
Reminding me that love and hope works to conquer
every tear.
Hope is not just a superficial feeling, but a powerful
fortress to escape or show me my way,
To transform the very darkness that plagues me through
the night and into a brand new day.

Hope is my sturdy, steadfast anchor, keeping me afloat
while truth is my guide,
Lifting my spirit and reminding me of who is in control
and that I am where peace will reside.
Unbreakable, boundless, eternally bright is the light of
the love when He is in my sight,
A glowing ember of hope leading me with His shining
radiant and light.

12. What is Hope?

Hope is a spark that burns with embers so iridescently
bright,
A flame that guides us through the dreadfulness of the
night.
It whispers courage when we're feeling confused and
low,
ultimately working to help our spirit continue to grow.

Hope is the essence of a dream that keeps us standing
strong,
Hope is the heartfelt melody of our peaceful inner song.
When shadows fall and darkness seems to be creeping
near,
Hope is the bright light that enables us to persevere.

It's not just whimsical wishing, but believing in
something really deep inside,
A strong power that helps us find a way to change
circumstances and turn the tide.
Hope lifts us up when we might otherwise settle for the

final fall,
Reminding us we can will ultimately with the love of
God overcome it all.

Hope is the dream that keeps us innately strong,
Hope is the heartfelt melody of our peaceful inner song.
When shadows fall and darkness seems to be creeping
near,
Hope is the bright light that enables us to persevere.

In moments of doubt, when our paths seem crooked and
somewhat unclear,
Hope is the compass that brings us close to our moments
of great cheer.
A soft, gentle promise, a resilient unforgettable embrace,
Showing us undeniable strength in every single creavous
of this place.

Hope is the delightful dream that keeps us full of faith
and strong,
Hope is the heartfelt melody of our peaceful inner song.
When shadows fall and darkness seems to be creeping
near,
Hope is the bright light that enables us to persevere.

13. A Culture of Hope

In the heart of the country, where shadows frolic play,
Hope dances freely, lighting the path in such a glorious
way.
With every new and picturesque sunrise, we are given a
new chance to rise,
Dreams take flight much like the elegant birds in the
skies.
Voices of many, directs a chorus so beautifully strong,
United in a common spirit, where all beings have a place
and feel they belong.
Through trials and struggles, we stand with a common
purpose side by side,
In this culture of hope, we all can unite in a common
purpose and take pride.
Each story an intricately woven thread in life's tapestry
being spun,
Together we make it through life's ups and downs and
flourish, together we are one.
Through laughter and tears, we find grow together,
nourish our soul, and find grace,

A culture of hope, a society of dreamers, all finding our
sacred space.
A Culture of Hope.

14. The Hope of a Selfless Mom

Your journey through life was difficult, yet full of love,
strength and hope.
The choice to hold on forever or let go was never in my
power to decide.
You happened to be my gift, so delicately intertwined
with strength and love.
Some pieces of me left with you on that fateful day, and
some of you will forever remain in me.

Now, I write to mend my brokenness and find the
courage to breathe again after you stopped.
That, sweet mom, seems almost impossible some days.
I have been given a burden that exceeds my strength and
understanding.
How can I leave you behind when you never once left
me?

This is our parting as mom and daughter, or at least how
we always knew it.

Instead of walking side by side in this life, I now trust
you to watch over my life while I live in the legacy of
yours.
Death, love, and finality all have completely new
meanings to me.
June the 9th will forever be etched in stone to create a
final chapter to such a beautiful story.

Many days I feel the need to lay down my shield and
surrender to the pain of grief.
Grief is not really a stage or stages for me, It is life's
harshest reality manifested into emotion- the loss of
someone,
I will never be the same.
It is life-changing, but do I really want to be?

It feels like pain.
It feels like agony.
It feels like an aching hurt.
But, most of all, it feels so bad that it almost feels good.
At least I am feeling at all.

The day you died mom, I found a new part of me called
grief which carries a rawness of emotions all entangled
with love, loss, and heartbreak.
Pain has silenced me on many occasions throughout this
journey, and my sincere hope is for you to know I miss

you and pray I am making you proud!

I cherish the words you left me in my letter; "Keep me in
your heart and our love will last forever."
Mom, my life has changed completely in a moment, but I
choose to believe that the beauty of love does not have to
be seen to be felt.
Peace will come, hope will endure, comfort will be found
and love will remain.

15. When Hope is Delicate.

Delicate yet strong as steel inside,
Hope bends but never breaks, it won't subside.
Fragile like a flame, yet burning with a fire so fierce,
Trembling yet unbroken, it will pierce.

Delicate yet strong as steel inside,
Hope bends but never breaks, it won't subside.
Fragile like a flame, yet burning with a fire so fierce,
Trembling yet unbroken, it will pierce.

Hope is a paradox, soft and completely unafraid,
Gentle as a soft feather, powerful as a mighty blade.
Wavering but standing, vulnerable but still strong,
A resilient melody, an unexplainable song.

Tender as a newly planted seedling, albeit still rooted
deep and true,
Never swaying with life's challenges, but growing strong
and new.

Fragile in its very essence, potent deep within its core,
Flowing with possibilities behind each proverbial closed
door.

Hope is a paradox, soft and completely unafraid,
Gentle as a soft feather, powerful as a mighty blade.
Wavering but standing, vulnerable but still strong,
A resilient melody, an unexplainable song.

Hope remains, hope sustains,
Fragile, potent - all the while breaking chains.

16. Hope's Energy

The energy hope brings dances, bravely igniting the
skies,
Multiple levels of courage arise.
Through valleys of doubt, hope flows like a roaring
stream,
Showing us the way to discover and fulfill our dream.
Hope is a spark, a flame that cannot extinguish or die,
It lifts those who believe high.
In moments of darkness, it glimmers bright,
A glow of hope and strength, our transforming light.
Hope brings the energy which allows dreams to come
true.

17. Ripples of Hope

In the stillness and luster of a snowy, winters' night, the
warmth of hope spreads through the air,
A ripple of hope travels through the galaxies straight
from the moon's soft glide.
Each wave echoes a promise, a dream pondering the
moment it may get to bloom,
Flashes of light fill the skies and cause shadows to
spatter the frozen tundra below.
In the heart of the blizzard, when despair can take hold,
Specific ripples of courage, brave stories must be shared.
With each blustery surge, we rise and we mend,
Hope is the current, and the ripples of hope create the
calm that will come.

18. My Love, My Hope

In this troubled world of doubt and relentless fear,
A young lady must hold on to what seems sincere.
My true love, my only hope, they both shine so bright,
I desire for them to guide me through my darkest night.

Like two sparrows amidst a hurricane,
You and I weathered every storm that came.
With you my heart is strong, my spirit seemed free,
Our love, our hope, they carried us.

When challenges tried to break us down,
We stood tall without even a weakened sound.
Our hope's a flame that cannot be dimmed,
Our love's strength comes from deep within.

No mountain high, no valley low,
Can stop the love that makes us grow.
Our hope's a lighthouse, burning so very true,
Showing us precisely what to do.

Like two sparrows amidst a hurricane,
You and I weathered every storm that came.
With you my heart is strong, my spirit seemed free,
Our love, our hope, they carried us,

The world was not sure we would make it, but our loved
said we would!